SWEET MOVIE

NATIONAL POETRY SERIES

The National Poetry Series was established in 1978 to
ensure the publication of five collections of poetry annually
through five participating publishers. The series is funded
annually by the Amazon Literary Partnership, William
Geoffrey Beattie, the Gettinger Family Foundation, Bruce
Gibney, HarperCollins Publishers, the Stephen and Tabitha
King Foundation, Padma Lakshmi, the Lannan Foundation,
Newman's Own Foundation, Anna and Olafur Olafsson,
Penguin Random House, the Poetry Foundation, Amy Tan
and Louis DeMattei, Amor Towles, Elise and Steven Trulaske,
and the National Poetry Series Board of Directors.

THE NATIONAL POETRY SERIES
WINNERS OF THE 2022 OPEN COMPETITION

Organs of Little Importance by Adrienne Chung
Chosen by Solmaz Sharif for Penguin Books

Tender Headed by Olatunde Osinaike
Chosen by Camille Rankine for Akashic Books

Survival Strategies by Tennison S. Black
Chosen by Adrienne Su for the University of Georgia Press

I Love Information by Courtney Bush
Chosen by Brian Teare for Milkweed Editions

Sweet Movie by Alisha Dietzman
Chosen by Victoria Chang for Beacon Press

SWEET MOVIE

P
O
E
M
S

ALISHA DIETZMAN

BEACON PRESS • BOSTON

Beacon Press
Boston, Massachusetts
www.beacon.org

Beacon Press books
are published under the auspices of
the Unitarian Universalist Association of Congregations.

26 25 24 23   8 7 6 5 4 3 2 1

This book is printed on acid-free paper that meets the uncoated
paper ANSI/NISO specifications for permanence as revised in 1992.

Composition by Kevin Barrett Kane at
Wilsted & Taylor Publishing Services

Cover art: Lauren Frances Evans, Grasp (2012), collage on paper, 12 in. × 9 in.
Image courtesy of the artist (www.laurenfrancesevans.com).

Library of Congress Cataloging-in-Publication Data is available for this title.

for Harrison

CONTENTS

FOREWORD

The poems in *Sweet Movie* are poems of perception and correspondence. As the poet writes in "The Margin of a Floating Structure": "Things are easier for me received." These poems use film and art to break open seeing so that what results are deeply insightful, capacious, and leaping poems that explore themes of faith, displacement, and love. These poems correspond with paintings such as *The Last Judgment* by Giotto di Bondone, a documentary about the Polygon test site, a Russell Lee photograph, and even lines from John Donne's "Holy Sonnets." The poet's mind opens up with the possibilities of language and leaping when perceiving things in the world, as if to say correspondence is a way to make and/or revise the self and thinking. Many of the poems in *Sweet Movie* begin by looking, are interrupted by self-reflection, and end with transformed perception.

Narrative leaps occur in many of the poems in *Sweet Movie*. The poet's own line from "Museum(s)" summarizes this marvelous book's poetics: "We're sieves, a series/of narrative leaps." The poems' cut-jumping and interstitial leaps seem influenced by and also reflect the speaker's childhood in Prague and in Arkansas and various other parts of the South. Such leaps may be a manifestation of the speaker's fragmented memories. As an example, in the first poem in the book, the text moves from preservation in a jar in the first line, to dreams, women's hairstyles that look like bombs, to the third stanza/line: "What gives us the right to listen to someone else's body?" The next stanza/line answers the question with another question masked as a declarative: "I don't know to whom these places belong." The flexibility of the word "places" sets the poem up for the next leap, to "vertices," which somehow leaps strangely and interestingly to "God." As a reader, I can imagine the next leap from God to "terrible light" and to the final question masked again as a declarative: "I want to know if we will imagine/the same light." These exciting leaps populate this entire book, and we readers get to witness the process of leaping, and the resulting electricity generated by the leaps.

Beyond the leaping, *Sweet Movie* simply contains beautiful writing. Take for instance, the poem "Nocturne (Slovakia)," in which nearly every line has its own personality: "*Some say I am from/_____, but really, I am from my mother*. I hold my/head out, dangerously, for decapitation. I disembark/with drunken neatness." Or pick any line from "Love Poem by the Light of Prague" to marvel at: "We're tundra, soft theater—/I hold you, I think—/grenadine all over my asymmetrical/mouth, you miss." Or from "Yet," a numbered poem that begins at the number "31": "There is a way we speak gently to animals/we'd like to keep: dogs, horses. In my mind God is always using that tone." In the poem "Thou Holdest Mine Eyes Waking," nearly every line makes the reader pause: "This city is more beautiful than swans hiding the water" or "The salt on the sidewalk is a soft shatter." The poems in *Sweet Movie* are wrought with beauty and being in the world.

Victoria Chang

1

LOVE POEM BY THE LIGHT OF A DOCUMENTARY ABOUT THE POLYGON TEST SITE

Almost anything can be preserved in a jar.

Mid-dusk dreams: women
with swollen hairstyles,
mirroring bombs.

What gives us the right to listen to someone else's body?

I don't know to whom these places belong.

At our vertices: God.

Imagine the most terrible light.
I want to know if we will imagine

the same light.

2

NOCTURNE (SLOVAKIA)

Praha hl.n.—Poprad-Tatry. 23:09—7:05

Night feels darker. Across the aisle two men eat a tin of meat, doll pink, the first nail-color allowed. I loved you when I said: *if Henry Darger drew us I'd be a small girl with male genitalia, and you'd be a small girl with male genitalia—we might be one girl.* The same flute-ribs, red-hood. Machete-ing our way through head-height flowers, dragon-like. This train is mostly yellow. If outside there is a forest, I do not know, but it is animal-less, if so, blood-let, and blood-lit, a few times. Now we rarely think about the absence of wolves. The last woman in my car exits ten minutes after four. I think about that serial killer picking victims based on a doorknob's looseness. I do not know where I am. Men sound louder. Most of the world might be this box. All the hands, blunt. And one man, his eyes so milk-blue, I see them for years. It's a holiday. *We are going home.* They are drinking, heavily. They are telling me jokes. *Some say I am from _____, but really, I am from my mother.* I hold my head out, dangerously, for decapitation. I disembark

with drunken neatness.

LOVE POEM BY THE LIGHT OF PRAGUE

We're dancing clumsily like parrots.
Every part of our bodies, tendon,

and nearing singular.
We're tundra, soft theater—

I hold you, I think—
grenadine all over my asymmetrical

mouth, you miss. Grenadine on my tongue,
and hipbone, somehow. We manage, listing

like arctic ships. A man screams,
slow-motion something

for no reason.

THE LAST JUDGMENT—GIOTTO DI BONDONE

Buon Fresco:

This cannot be undone easily.

Organs like quicklime.
This they'd call sublime, later:
vast/terror.

Hung by hair, by tongue, some
spilt-out, over-ripe and ever-young,
like water.

Do not   look at me   that way.

Nothing of ours will ever be slaked.

But oiled and spit-turned,
salt-pigs, fig-eyes, leaking,

I suppose we make each other hungry.

YET

with some language drawn from part two of
The 120 Days of Sodom

31. We start at *corrupt.*

32. There is a way we speak gently to animals
    we'd like to keep: dogs, horses.
    In my mind God is always using that tone.

33. Somehow my skin is still cold. I'd like to say I want nothing.
    Want appears three times here and tastes better
    the more you say it:

34. *Want.* In my dreams I force-feed God to sharks.
    This will need to be described.
    I thought the sharks would be more excited by the blood.

35. I had been led to believe we are mostly instinctual.

36. I wander over bodies in my mind. I am bored
    by even the word bodies—
    they are,

37. and longsuffering, sweetish.
    Perhaps best described as small towns.

38. I will wonder if what I imagine is a sin
    for the rest of my life.

39. Maybe this is shock value.
    Awe should be reserved for God, only:
    I've heard this suggested. We are lonely

40. like pianos. I've heard this suggested.
    There is nothing beautiful

41. without shame, and almost nothing
    without shame. Sometimes I wish I could give you
    all this shame. You'll never feel

42. all this beautiful shame.

43. In order for this to become a prayer
    I need only to change the address,

44. but not yet.

45. In the 1975 film adaptation,
    one of the four main men claims:
    you see how sensitive I am to the value of things.

46. In order for this to become a prayer
    I need only to change the address.

47. I call you Lord, God—forgive me my _____.
    Some variant of I am this terrible

48. ornament. *Confession*: I will think of you forever,

49. a little.

HEALING "LAYING ON OF HANDS" CEREMONY——RUSSELL LEE

1st photograph

A man flails. His white eyes in snake-neck head, white,
again I say, as if *rejoice.* A girl on her knees. The other men,
There would be a human smell: salt, as with you, though
with you, a little sap. Their hands cut the air. One, his blur,
come out spirit, like. I notice the ceiling is low. I notice
the girl has a ribbon curled around her hair. I notice God

2nd photograph

Another girl, on her head, a crown of hands. I notice
what do they say, *sensuous details.* Fleeting   small dress
Belt buckle like a jawline. Jawlines. No higher resolution.
Once a man pulled me from the service, claimed he saw
God all over me like milk, and why was I *so afraid
of God*, of his hands, here,   and elsewhere. Why did I *fear*

dogwood.

does not let us go.

I imagine light blue.

mercy.

MUSEUM(S)

Did you not pour me out like milk?

On floor 2 an attendant listens to bombs going off all day.

Outside Tallinn in the wasp   fields,
shaking: a caved building like a valve.

A blue forest with men picking mushrooms.

The band on the commuter ferry sings *PARTY ROCK*
to violent applause. We're sieves, a series

of narrative leaps.
A middle-aged woman dancing

like smoke.

God has such mercy on us.

MUSEUM(S)

Did you not pour me out like milk?

Gustavs Klucis' lithe cutouts.

Bayonet. Ruby.

Hollow-bodied   woman in the photograph. Bruised canister.

Directions (in case) and little red
fire alarms.

> Once I screamed at you to know I am capable of screaming
> when called upon. That in urgent situations, I might could.

Anyway, nobody reads history anymore.

A hogtied horse.

Are you interested in violence or are you bored?
Both *yeses*, immoral.

> I have heard that even with a gun to your head,
> your consent is yours.

Folk skirt, floating. No legs. No waist.

Maybe 30 dresses, I can't count, in found-florals,
without comment.

The marble heads of dozens in state.

Man eating pearls, possibly.

Sacrificial vertebrae. Ration.

A single Vermeer.

Klucis, again. His long-armed,   beautiful Lenin.

Gustavs Klucis is shot by the NKVD in winter.
I think about this for days. That nothing saves some of us.

More paintings: abstract hydrangeas
in front of a house, burning.

In the video installation, a woman: *the clients like all cavities.*

Print of stacked cabbages,
from a distance.

A wet pane of glass and a lilac
growing back through the window.

THOU HOLDEST MINE EYES WAKING

I pray now mostly out of fear.
Thou holdest mine eyes waking.

This city is more beautiful than swans hiding the water.

The salt on the sidewalk is a soft shatter.
Our January hands

bright like meat, in front rooms where we shake
off coats, white like fox bellies. In us,

there are elaborate structures. I feel the thicket of you,
close, warm. And the blue background of the nightly news

is a holy sonnet of bodies battered, badly, and maybe after
looking God in the eye. The nightly news spills over your neck,

tentacle of light. We are deep-sea creatures in our dark.
You are eerie beside me. I remember a man

at a party who said to me: *here you are, drunk,* like it was some
miracle—and then: *I've lost God.* He said because God

is a God who asks, a God who wanted everything dead
a few times over, commands ash, and utter consuming,

and none allowed left. Even the animals burned.

LOVE POEM BY THE LIGHT OF THE REFRIGERATOR

If you open the door, the light
blue light is watery as girls in those
limp posters, overhead. I am listening
to your memory and it sounds like
UNLIMITED ACCESS. I call your name,
tenderly. We live in a world
with few headboards, left.
Their little decency
offends me, anyway/anyway
I call your name, tenderly.
I spit in the sink. The near miss
of this always makes my hands cold,

loose, and then I feel *few*—that's it,
that's what I wanted to say: few.

GOSHA RUBCHINSKIY X THE POEM

Beauty is boring. Here it looks like chewing gum.
The inside of a dog's ear.

This couplet is a capsule collection
made of new capitalism and seed beads

ripped off a late-80s clutch. The gray strings
left behind are sad and lonely

as current-day prophets, weeping
while they brush their teeth. Salt

all in their throats. God is never enough.
God is never enough.

My prayers grow bitter.

There is a forest just outside the city
where streams circle weird little islands.

I know that what I want is not to forget.
There is a glamour in saying I want to forget,

but I am consumed like a dog by the dreamless
dead in the same forest, and anxious.

Maybe some of them have their own weird little islands
and are in death, shiny and wet and gorgeous,

only metal and leather left, like robots.
This is about the living, though

responding to casting calls,
telling us their dogs are afraid

of separation, and anxious.
One boy plays the piano in an auditorium,

another kicks a hole in the wall of an empty house.
Each tells us the history of his town

as introduction. *An altar of boys*,
Gosha calls them, in a pre-Soviet church/gym:

it was like how you could see the faces of saints.

GOSHA RUBCHINSKIY X TIMUR NOVIKOV

In the image it appears to be summer. June
wanting the land with its whole green mouth.

Boy models lean like Baroque furniture,
objects for fainting. History, a bad streak, a thin line

like their lips, mostly closed, but in some images,
slightly parted—small pink, half-no,

which can mean a thousand words, though,
I think most often: *why*.

In *Untitled* by Timur Novikov
a tiny, literal tractor discovers the surreal,

and it is a field that swims.
Everything is so delicate in this world,

I imagine God would be a spoon.
Even the infinite rendered a girl, snow.

WE DID NOT KNOW MUCH ABOUT THAT CITY

Outside the train, backyards. Bare clotheslines strung
only with clothespins. I wonder if it is going to rain.

Outside the train, a rabbit skin, oddly clean.

Night spreads sweeter than anise in the city
where we are going, where a man sits with three shots
of absinthe, the sharp green of copper, after.
And we remember that there were three shots—
because why so many for one man and in a row.

Outside the train, children wearing gloves.

Outside the train, blank townscapes where once
they lined men against a wall. There reaches a point
when counting becomes a waste of time.

Night spreads sweeter than anise in the city
where we are going, in its parks by the river
where it is dark, deep dark, as space is dark,
under a moon that is light, is barely light,
as God is light. And God is a smocked collar
over our literal heart, is our sadness
in spilled things—glasses of water, memorials.

I tell you what happened is not unique,
but it is particular. And I like particular.
I like careful. I like every word thought through,
like when Žižek shakes his hands in the video, says
it was *some maybe probably genocide*.
Careful *maybe*. Careful *probably*. Careful *genocide*.

Night spreads sweeter than anise in the city
where we have arrived, and over a table
that is a little too narrow, we agree
to give up. Which is intimacy, maybe.
And intimacy is also houseplants,
the manner in which curtains touch sills.

We say alright. We say thy will.
And all of this, quiet. And all of this, running out of air
like pool floats, like pale blue. Like us, if we cut
even the smallest holes in certain parts of our bodies.

DUŠAN MAKAVEJEV'S *W.R.:*
MYSTERIES OF THE ORGANISM

In the end, Vladimir Ilyich beheads Milena with an ice skate.
Milena's head tells us *he's romantic—*
with his sad, important hands.

We're romantic in the same way.
At some point as in all movies,
there is despair on the faces of the band.

Milena's death is not strictly political.
She is not sock-white on a battlefield.
There are no trumpets.

I know the primary mystery of the organism
is not Milena's head looking for a body
like a doll. There is something larger.

I like to imagine her anyway as a ghost
of a fictional character, who dies like we often do,
for satire. I know how important it is to be part of a narrative.

LOVE POEM BY TRAIN LIGHT

Notes in the margins of St. Augustine's *Confessions*:

Electro-pop. Nonlinear. Forests.

Failed bombshells periodically found
under blueberries.

Three times I mistook a city for a city in mornings
bright as mouthwash.

     And contained within—devastation.

The sugar on your fingers.

The scent of your hair like nettle.

3

THE MARGIN OF A FLOATING STRUCTURE

To speak plainly, we met eating tomatoes.
To speak plainly.

        A 24-hour street of flowerstands in Riga.

We fought. You allowed an amber necklace, nothing else.
The picture of this hour lamblike, post-development.
My nakedness a (little) theory. You imagine
winter. Birch. Looking at me.

Once a year in Arkansas my father sits in a house
returning to dust.

In the Europe of my childhood my mother is handed irises.
I know they have wondered why they came,
but have never left, live on a street still   with lindens.

Memory, an island on the river. The balcony
of the theater speaking hotly how he ate his lover.
The attendant touches our coats like I have your mouth
an hour before.

This is a strange continent.
I tell you there is a point of no return.
A shop selling only lamps that have lit wars.

The man wraps our purchase in plastic. Outside,
(a) night.

        This is not a moral object, the poem.

Walking the Tiergarten my father tells me about the 80s, here.
He tells me his favorite memory of his father: skinning a deer

,together,
back home.   An hour's drive past Memphis, it quiets.

       How can I be without border?

The lonely hairclips of an empress. Cherry liqueur
and a little theory. A bucket of rusting,
Soviet-era pins.

Tourists wondering how it all became so cliché,
what they wanted   untouched.

What has been untouched?:

    ON BINGE, LOCAL LADY RUBS BODY AGAINST.
    Groups of young boys roam the gardens newly dark.
    The scent of onions on the pillow.
    In the conventional manner, we unclothe.

In Riga we watch a woman laden with flowers, fat roses—
small dogs, you tell me.

Next-door's party leaks through the walls.

You make me watch *L'Avventura*.

Monica Vitti,
soft, unnaturally beautiful
as the snapped neck of a rabbit.

I make you watch *Hundstage*.

I feel as if I remember the lawns, and rooms.
Man in dumb yellow shirt.
The one, too, who hits her, unsimulated,
the one who says: *you're like all the other bitches.*

Things are easier for me received.

Once a year in Arkansas my father kills snakes in a house
returning to dust.

My grandfather dies loosening his tie in a church corridor;
looking. Out the door where he smoked with the elders:
a famous highway, a long green.

In another dream my father sits with his father
in the house returning to dust.

I know my doubt disappoints him.

My sisters and I tan our legs. Our   appliance-white
                                        art-history torsos,

inside,   on the kitchen floor.   Trash,
splayed   over every visible surface.

Have you accepted Jesus Christ as your Lord and Savior?
I do not mind anymore my low church,
how unwieldy the many factors like a horse.

Near home, in the Europe of my childhood: at the ossuary.
The tourists wonder how it all became so *touched*.
And why does everyone have the same ideas, they ask.

Come with me—

Habsburg park design. Somewhere beneath our   meeting?
—how do you say this with more breath—
a plague burial.   All the rain in the air.

God loves you and offers a wonderful plan for your life.

On a bus nearly to Russia,
on a beach with a bunker. Cucumbers.
Vodka that tastes like the palm of a hand; simultaneity.

The parquet in the summer palace
is as much evidence as anything
God loves us.

Sweetness in the porcelain,   belly-up.
You could break with your jaw,   *easy*.

Those display-case   milkmaids dressed in fingernails.

Long walk back to the sea and an interlude of trees.
Lost looking for a grave in the birch, like nakedness,

the flower in a fish,
cut a certain way.   I can't stop looking at you,
                       to speak plainly. I can't stop looking.

LOVE POEM BY THE LIGHT OF ETERNITY AND A REALITY TV SHOW ABOUT LOVE

Women radiate through the medium in wet-look
dresses like grass in the morning.

Women float lonely on the surface of the pool, pool floats
occasionally touching. My beloved,

I love that word, so Shulamite, presses his forehead to mine.
He tells me about the time he first read *the birds!—the birds!*

What does it matter?

STERN—MARLENE DUMAS

A necklace—that's a joke. Photographic material reveals
marks, in this rendering rope-like.[1] In appearance.
The image is not glossy but it is erotic in lieu of sexual.
The first time I heard a coyote I thought it was a murder.[2]
In *A Few Howls Again*, Ulrike Meinhof resurrects
to tell us: *my kind of violence made people nervous.*[3]
I have been considering that I am not good for many years,
but lately it comes upon me, as we are come upon.
Naturally I am in every bar wondering about interior lives.
I like imagining tragedy. Who doesn't? A man confesses,
I can't hear to what; it's all tonal, like movies
where there are crows. One of my sisters calls daily
to say she wants to kill a woman.[4]

1   But merely marks from the redacted rope (with which Ulrike
    Meinhof killed herself, or   ).
2   I am the kind of person who hears a coyote for the first time and
    thinks it is a murder. I am the kind of person who hears a coyote
    for the first time.
3   In another frame from Silvia Kolbowski's *A Few Howls Again*,
    the text "she was unrealistic in the face of police brutality" floats
    above Meinhof's body.
4   Will you forgive me?

ALFA—MARLENE DUMAS

Alfa is the name of an elite military unit. I say this because *Alfa*
is not the name of the woman, dead, we are led by so much
to believe. We are led by so much to believe. The way a sleeve
slips, the woman is on the floor. Dumas paints
because she is *a religious woman.*[1] Perhaps I am good
at the grand scheme of things for the same reason.[2]
In every article on the siege, shock: the woman
likely committed to her own dying; we can't know for sure—
Dumas prefers allusion. White-lipped, luminous
as gasoline, what does the woman say to the theater ceiling,

looking down at all that desire?[3]

---

1   (She *believes in eternity.*)
2   Or I have tried.
3   In the end it was inevitable that I still believe in eternity.

LUCY—MARLENE DUMAS

This one's dead, too spoke darkly like crime show
dialogue. Ulrike Meinhof, *Unknown*, St. Lucy—
lambs/lions/lambs/lions.[1] Innocence is hard to keep.[2]
I tell you I think not one of us has it, not one of us.
That's critical to the narrative no one finds
in the end. I'll be somewhere, to a degree, etherized,
and eating peaches. Dumas's *Lucy* is Caravaggio's
martyred Lucy, with all original features: slit neck
and sweetness.[3] To me her leaking is more his *Mary
Magdalen in Ecstasy*. Their seeking, wild throats,
Lord. I do not even know where I want to be buried.[4]

1 *Unknown* references the woman in Dumas's *Alfa*.
2 My parents are missionaries. We are all, all of us, *short of the
glory of God*.
3 Caravaggio's *Burial of St. Lucy* resembles a bowl of ice cream.
4 Marlene Dumas calls herself *a woman who does not know where
she wants to be buried* (in the original, *anymore*).

MIRACLE(S)

with a line from Yeats

Some people do not even fear The Apocalypse.
. . . .
Cinematic   fast-food.
. . . .
Exposed little flesh.
. . . .
Caught in that sensual music all neglect.
. . . .
The faith of the saints. In heat, *Lord*, in drought.
. . . .
St. Lucy: her eyes cut out.
. . . .
Certain metaphor, obviously.
. . . .
The absence of any possible metaphor
at times. That presence.
. . . .
No baptism to me in Malick's saturation;
baptism as present in the cumshot,
I do not even watch.
I say that to make the budding theologians
. . . .
angry at the house party.

. . . .

(The miracle is immanence.)

. . . .

Violinists.

. . . .

4

HOLY SONNETS

1. Thou hast made me I dare not move my dim eyes.

I know enough about the interiors of cars to get by.
Some aluminum terms like axle, infinity.

My mother told me nobody can be trusted
if they say they love you.

2. *As due thine image I wilt.*

Yieldingly, sometimes.

A good movie is a movie where nobody knows anything
but the end, and throughout, the nature of everything
nobody knows, loops, a constant. It is warm.
A woman swims in the Mediterranean;

her small, naked mouth and eternity.

3. *Oh! Holy discontent. Some fruit, night-scouting.*

Lord, you did not leave me. If nothing else remains, let this.

4. *Like doom, grace.*

I said I know enough to get by.
I know where the gun is kept and how to use it;
this surprises people sometimes.

I know where the money is, too, and the keys.
I know what we can't outrun, and I know when to give up
and reveal the mourning tongues of my arms

and like it   some. I listen.

5. *I am a little new land burn me.*

I tell you what—
I'd like to let you cut me in the courtyard
where I am weakest and sweetest.

And one day I will understand myself
in a grand-historical sense, I know.

6. *Unjoint my fear and purg'd I leave the world.*

It was a long drive the time I was lost, somewhat,
in Wyoming and listening to the voices. All night.
I kept the driver awake with questions—
How can you tell when the wind will shift
and turn the fire? And overwhelm you, and then?
What recourse? Are you ever afraid or mostly only
very well-trained?

It is important for me to know if anyone panics.

7. *Let me mourn a space.*

8. *Apparent in us. Then turn.*

I am always saying every Susanna among every Elder,
brush-*stroked*: enough. Plenty. One leg in the linden water,
enough. June, enough.

Only when the beautiful women I know
tore their metaphorical clothes, pleading,
Lord, come for us,

I did not want to go.

9. *And mercy being mercy if thou wilt forget.*

By some metrics I am good
but I am only interested in metrics formed in blood.

10. Thou art pleasures, soonest.

It is difficult to explain I do not hate my shame.
I return to it as a dog.

While the assembled on both sides cover their eyes,
I want only for you to call me *garden*,

garden.   And yours,   wholly as holy.

11. O let me then his strange love.

In the movie where the only known thing is the end,
men speak freely of apocalypse. A goat walks over the sand.
The woman rises from the water. Suddenly modest,
her arms form sacred symbols.

12. Weakness, swallow, and wonder.

13. My idolatry a sign of rigor.

I want to believe a good start is knowing,
but it is the world's last night,
and when asked to get the money,
I have no excuse.

You count it and cry.

14. Yet dearly I love you, imprison me.

Lost in Wyoming that time, the night-cold and the driver
explaining the mechanics of dying
by fire: superheated air

you draw into yourself like touch.

15. Wilt, thou slain.

In the movie where the only known thing is the end
men speak freely of the apocalypse.

Occasionally they call the apocalypse the name of the woman
who swam in the water, who covered herself.

It's a sad movie, really.

16. Thy kingdom this Lamb.

There was violence even in the scene with fruit.
A man licks her spilt face and we know then he loved her.

LOVE POEM BY THE LIGHT OF THE DESERT

I didn't expect the desert, its longform.
We took ourselves to water.

I cannot say everything was beautiful,
but mostly, yes;

I am grateful for the names of God
we are allowed to speak, and the hidden.

We didn't intend to see them fucking among the trees,
as deer to me, in my particular way.

I have rejected certain discourses,
I have accepted certain discourses.

A man you work with tells me he knows
everything there is to know about religion.

I practice a certain docility in my discourses.
I tell you again, again, the desert,

something dead already, resurrected: the tightly metered
voice calling out kidnappings, the weather,

mildly apocalyptic all June.
In the river you are cold in my mouth.

LOVE POEM BY YELLOW LIGHT

July: loose   dress.
Outside the town, the sage on fire
smells like sugar, money.

That man you work with burning
sage, dousing sage, tells me he knows
everything there is to know about religion,

and none of it good.

We are in a bar on Taco Tuesday.
Beside him someone keeps saying softly
he's killed a cougar. Beside him: yellow

vinyl reflects yellow. Uneasy glasses.
Michel Pastoureau devotes himself
entirely to the study of color:

first and foremost a social phenomenon.

Yellow is the least loved color, in most socials,
per Pastoureau. My hands slide down my glass,
coldblooded as airports.

The man tells me he's going on a date.
He does not know the woman. He tells me
they will undress together and run

through the rooms of her quiet
house   somewhere in Idaho:
two pale verses.

TWO PALE VERSES

My mother asks if I'm reading Jeremiah. A man
on break from Winco watches me comb my hair.

DUŠAN MAKAVEJEV'S *LOVE AFFAIR, OR THE CASE OF THE MISSING SWITCHBOARD OPERATOR*

The criminologist addresses us directly and specifically:

A murderer will often stare long and hard at the motionless body.

Izabela, breathless and nude at the window.
Izabela, milk over her breasts. Izabela and Ahmed
on a bed, looking at the other. Izabela and Ahmed
in a bed, looking at the other. Eating honey.
Pressed against the shower curtain like a memory.
The examiner forms a V beneath Izabela's breasts.
He fans her brain into a forest.

The human body is made up of an enormous number of substances.

Strawberries, TV, and God. Too much to recount.
Still, of course we try.

The criminal always seeks to make a "leap into the void."

This strikes me as overwrought but accurate.
What interests me, for example, is the loneliness
of the evidence: her shoes. A sundress.

BIG LOVE VOL. 1

I like these women who do not share my faith.
They are called *transgressive* by a critic,
favorably so. They have a faith, and it is practice.
Not my faith, but near my practice. In chapel, a girl
beside me, soft as an eel, says she wants to *die soon,*
or *come, Lord, come.* Her absence already a presence.
My absence no good absence unable as I am, to let go
of presence. A man I serve beer says it's sweet I believe.
Around my neck, St. Thomas who doubted God.
I still wear St. Thomas, though I no longer doubt God.
I nearly left St. Thomas on the ferry to Finland.
I was so drunk that night and afraid. I drank anise?
liqueur on the cold deck. I liked that water
you can't tell from night, the store full of perfume.
Someone allowing their scream to float.

BIG LOVE VOL. 2

In the final episode the women exchange
meaningful glances in a small car.

Women are episodes of exchange.
Small car moves like a glance.

The desert is final.
One of the women wears a scarf;

the long sleeve of another, *Lord*.

BIG LOVE VOL. 3

Collection of women in white wandering the dust.

I am fervent, and attached to fervor.
I am doubtful, and attached to doubt. The dust
soiling, I   consider the hems.

The women are small-scale, stretches of empty
committed to the large-scale: the long haul
of being on this beautiful little earth

like a gas station, in the heat   half vision.
All the stripped metal gone white.

LOVE POEM WITHOUT LIGHT

I should write more about America and us naked in a river.

You called me a coward as you took off your clothes.
Not wanting to be a coward, I took off my clothes.

> The midnight of a night slipping
> over rotting flowers.

But we were naked in the day—
that is why we are not cowards—

an old man watched us, saying
he wanted us to know we were beautiful.

The rotting came later, long past you floating
on the water. Some parts darkening; your hair.

We went to a bar and found three girls in dresses
drinking cokes. Even from a distance they were a certain

revelation. Their ankles so wonderful and cold,
yes, cold, in the slow-coming dark. It was a desert.

At home we drank again in the front yard.
We didn't know what the flowers were, Magnolia,

maybe—no, not here—but the smell was familiar,
perhaps it was the death. Our insect hands ran over each other.

LOVE POEM BY THE LIGHT OF THE DOCUMENTARY
*HOLY GHOST PEOPLE/*ARS POETICA

The scent of your hair like nettle *and my hands dripped with myrrh.*
The scent of your hair like nettle *and my hands dripped with myrrh.*
The scent of your hair like nettle *and my hands dripped with myrrh.*
The scent of your hair like nettle *and my hands dripped with myrrh.*
The scent of your hair like nettle.

Do not write about sin—sin belongs to belief.

LOVE POEM BY THE LIGHT OF SOMETHING OBVIOUS

A candle. A fire. There's nothing wrong
with common side effects. We drove west
holding hands like criminals.

The walls of motels the color of sage and movies,
but mostly tents and cold meat. The grease
on your mouth and breath, hardening.

The woods of your neck

in that early

green winter.

Supplication is a word that feels sacred.
The desert, always an archetype
in fine form: lonely

man bent on violence,
like lonely men, bent on violence.
Your one point is always depravity.

Hear me out—I'm saying
in Ellensburg, drunk, again:
there's actually no plan, after all.

I think in a formal way we're agreeing: God
was here, once. There are too many
starved expressions like love

of the holy, or only
looking. The seeking splits
too many throats open.

THE LAST JUDGMENT—GIOTTO DI BONDONE

Fresco-Secco:

There is a disinterest in lasting:

we say we were not made for this;
we do not have long-haul bodies,
we peel and drip, yet don't drain.

You can't behead eternity—

so we scratch its surface.

And by surface I mean your skin
with my free hand. I mean your mouth
when I can. I mean your head.
I pull your hair

like wheat.

ACKNOWLEDGMENTS

Many thanks to the following journals for publishing poems (or early versions of poems) appearing in *Sweet Movie*: *Bat City Review*, *Beloit Poetry Journal*, *Chicago Review*, *Changes*, *Denver Quarterly*, *DIAGRAM*, *Hotel*, *The Iowa Review*, *jubilat*, *The Massachusetts Review*, *Mississippi Review*, *Nashville Review*, *New South*, *Ninth Letter*, *Pain*, *Pleiades*, and *Poetry Northwest*.

Poems from this manuscript also appeared in the chapbook *Slow Motion Something For No Reason* (Factory Hollow Press, 2022), which was the editors' choice selection for the Tomaž Šalamun Prize.

I am additionally grateful to the University of St. Andrews—particularly my PhD advisor, Gavin Hopps—the US-UK Fulbright Commission, and the Jeffrey Rubinoff Sculpture Park for supporting my academic work, which animates my creative work.

Thank you to everyone at the Rebecca Swift Foundation for supporting me both as a poet and a person. I will always remember your kindness.

I would be nowhere without the love of my wonderful parents, Terry and Alethea Brown. To both of you, thank you; if you take nothing away but this, know that the example of your faith sustained—and sustains—my faith.

Thank you to my sisters and brother: Amanda Brown, Bethany Focht, and Nathanael Brown. I am so lucky to have each of you.

Thank you to a few people who aren't here to see this: my four strange and perfect grandparents, Alois Holub, Annie-Virginia Eich, Buddy and Bethyl Brown, and my father-in-law, Dave Dietzman. I'm deeply grateful for the time I received with each of you.

Thank you to longtime friends and early readers: Emily Trča, you are everywhere here, and in so many ways; Jamie Janus, I hope no one else ever gets a tattoo because of my poetry; Leslie Sainz, *Sweet Movie* would likely not exist without your encouragement.

Thank you to the MFA faculty at the University of Wisconsin-Madison for giving me a chance that changed my life. Thank you, too, to my MFA cohort, especially Carolyn Orosz, for your friendship and care with my work.

Thank you to those directly involved in bringing *Sweet Movie* into the world: the National Poetry Series and Beacon Press.

I will never have the perfect words to thank Victoria Chang for selecting my manuscript and believing in its possibility, but I will be grateful for the rest of my life.

Lastly, Harrison Dietzman, thank you for everything, always.

NOTES

I took the title of this book, *Sweet Movie*, from Dušan
Makavejev's 1974 film, also titled *Sweet Movie*.

The Polygon test site referenced in "Love Poem by the
Light of a Documentary About the Polygon Test Site" is the
Semipalatinsk Nuclear Test Site in Kazakhstan, formerly the
Soviet Union's most active nuclear test site.

In "*The Last Judgment*—Giotto di Bondone," *Buon Fresco* refers
to a manner of applying paint to wet plaster to form a long-
lasting, highly durable fresco.

"Yet" draws some language from both the Marquis de Sade's *120
Days of Sodom* and Pier Paolo Pasolini's 1975 film adaptation,
Salò, or the 120 Days of Sodom.

"*Healing 'Laying On of Hands' Ceremony*—Russell Lee" engages
with two 1946 photographs taken by Lee at a Pentecostal church
service in Lejunior, Harlan County, Kentucky.

In the first "Museum(s)," the epigraph is from Job 10:10 (NKJV).

In the second "Museum(s)," I interact with the life and art of Latvian artist Gustavs Klucis. Despite his active participation in the Soviet Communist movement, the NKVD executed Klucis in February 1938. The line "the clients like all cavities" is from Liina Siib's *Averse Body*. The epigraph is also from Job 10:10 (NKJV). This poem is for Klucis.

The title "Thou Holdest Mine Eyes Waking" appears in Psalm 77:4 (KJV). All other scriptural references in the manuscript are from the New King James Version, with the exception of this title, which I took from a King James devotional book that belonged to my grandmother, Annie-Virginia.

"Gosha Rubchinskiy x the Poem" interacts with the short film *Journey to Kaliningrad*, which documents the attempts of three young men to be cast in one of Rubchinskiy's shows.

"Gosha Rubchinskiy x Timur Novikov" interacts with photographs documenting a capsule collection from the designer. In this capsule collection, Rubchinskiy employs images from the artist Timur Novikov. Novikov painted more than one work called *Untitled*, but in the poem I am referencing a particular *Untitled* from 1988 featuring a small tractor and a yellow sky.

"Dušan Makavejev's *W.R.: Mysteries of the Organism*" interacts with Makavejev's 1971 film.

In "*The Margin of a Floating Structure*," I drew the title and the italicized fragment in the twenty-second line from Julia Kristeva's *Powers of Horror: An Essay on Abjection*. Other italicized fragments draw from *Have You Heard of the Four*

Spiritual Laws?, the booklet by Bill Bright, and Ulrich Seidl's 2001 film, *Hundstage*.

In "Love Poem by the Light of Eternity and a Reality TV Show About Love," the final italicized fragment reading *"the birds!— the birds!"* appears in *Moby Dick*.

"Stern—Marlene Dumas" interacts with Dumas's painting of Ulrike Meinhof, *Stern*, as well as Silvia Kolbowski's *A Few Howls Again*. Dumas's painting was inspired by the famous photograph of Meinhof in the magazine *Stern*, which also served as inspiration for Gerhard Richter's three versions of *Dead*, part of his *October 18, 1977* series.

"Alfa—Marlene Dumas" interacts with Dumas's painting *Alfa*. The italicized language in *"Alfa"* is drawn from Marlene Dumas's manifesto of sorts, "Women and Painting." The woman represented in *"Alfa"* is either a victim or a perpetrator of the 2002 Dubrovka Theater siege. Some hints in the painting suggest the latter.

"Lucy—Marlene Dumas" interacts with Dumas's painting *Lucy* as well as Caravaggio's *Mary Magdalen in Ecstasy* and his *Burial of Saint Lucy*. The second footnote in *"Lucy"* borrows from Romans 3:23 (NKJV). The italicized language in the fourth footnote comes from Dumas's "Measuring Your Own Grave."

The fourth line in "Miracle(s)" appears in William Butler Yeats's "Sailing to Byzantium." The poem is also indebted, in a way, to the films of Terrence Malick.

Each of the sixteen section headings in "Holy Sonnets" uses language drawn from the numerically corresponding sonnet in John Donne's *Holy Sonnets*.

"Love Poem by Yellow Light" draws on the work of Michel Pastoureau.

"Dušan Makavejev's *Love Affair, or the Case of the Missing Switchboard Operator*" interacts with Makavejev's 1967 film.

"*Big Love* Vol. 1," "*Big Love* Vol. 2," and "*Big Love* Vol. 3" all engage with the HBO series by the same name.

The repeated, italicized line in "Love Poem by the Light of the Documentary *Holy Ghost People*/Ars Poetica" comes from Song of Solomon 5:5 (NKJV).

In "*The Last Judgment*—Giotto di Bondone," *Fresco Secco* refers to a manner of applying paint to dry plaster to form a more alterable but less enduring fresco.